KALAHARI

JACQUES GILLIÉRON

KALAHARI

NEW
HOLLAND

First published in 1989 in the UK by
New Holland (Publishers) Ltd
37 Connaught Street, London W2 2AZ

ISBN 1 85368 086 9

Editor: Jean-François Godet
Jacket design: Studio Editions André Delcourt
Typeset by Desktop Design cc
Colour separations by Berger & Fatio, Denges/Lausanne
Printed in Switzerland by the Nouvelle Imprimerie Courvoisier,
La Chaux-de-Fonds
Bound by Mayer & Soutter, Renens/Lausanne

Foreword

Those regions of the globe as yet unexplored are becoming ever more rare. This is a sad state of affairs, not only for the traveller, but also for the naturalist. Our century offers us a thousand-and-one ways to travel at low cost to all corners of our planet, but nothing succeeds in quenching the thirst for discovery like wide open spaces. Nature enthusiasts, in particular, are always searching for these remote, unspoilt regions, and perhaps that is why I set out to explore the African continent.

I journeyed first to the west, to the Sahel countries, and then to the east, where I roamed the Serengeti in Tanzania. During my travels, I indeed managed to discover patches of virgin soil, regions unviolated by progress. However, it was only when I entered the great wilderness of Botswana that I realized that our earth can still boast natural expanses that stretch over thousands of square kilometres. Although during my other travels I had certainly discovered many such areas of limited extent, I must admit that this was the first time I had ever experienced such a vast uninhabited stretch and such a splendid natural wonder as that which exists in Botswana and, more specifically, in the Kalahari.

Situated in the very heart of Africa, away from the great sea and air routes, the Kalahari has virtually been forgotten by the outside world. In an era when one thinks one has experienced everything, it is comforting to discover that a whole slice of the African continent is still an untouched and unknown paradise. It is in this spirit of wonder and admiration that I have selected — from numerous photographs taken during three expeditions — the pictures for this book.

Of course, it is not really possible to describe fully the complexity of this unknown corner of Africa within the confines of a book of this size. I had to edit the collection knowing full well that this meant offering a limited view, and for this reason I have chosen to focus mainly on the wildlife of the Kalahari, the fauna peculiar to this remote sanctuary. All the pictures in this book were taken in Botswana, although strictly speaking the Kalahari includes parts of Namibia, South Africa and, in an ecological sense, Angola, Zambia and Zimbabwe as well.

If I am biased about Botswana, it is because of its unique situation, its isolation from the great metropolises, and the richness and diversity of its fauna. I also found the country to be welcoming and its inhabitants warm-hearted. Anyone who has travelled independently, without the help of tourist organizations, will know from experience that expeditions such as these are no small ventures. In Botswana, I was never made to feel like an outsider and I never once felt insecure. By nature, the people of Botswana are tolerant and peaceful. This young republic is politically neutral; in fact, many observers have likened it to Switzerland. The country has very little human conflict, perhaps because it is so sparsely populated: in an area of over 570 000 square kilometres (that is, a little larger than France) there are barely a million inhabitants.

It goes without saying that when one enters a region where there is no formal communications infrastructure, one must pay a great deal of attention to detail when preparing for the trip. I shall not bore the reader with a full list of the material I took along, although in order to answer some of the many queries I receive, I will provide information about the photographic equipment I used.

Unlike many photographers, I did not worry unduly about the weight or bulk of my equipment, although I preferred to leave behind the numerous gadgets that some people tend to load themselves down with when travelling to similar regions. For most of my expeditions, I drove a four-wheel-drive vehicle which conveniently served as a bed, a kitchen, a library and as shelter against the merciless Kalahari sun. Sometimes the car became a despised object because, despite all its special capabilities, it tended to break down and get stuck when travelling over rough terrain.

Because I wasn't limited in terms of weight, I was able to take all the photographic equipment I required for documenting the Kalahari. For my first two trips, I made use of 35-mm and large-format (60 mm x 60 mm) cameras. However, I soon realized that the latter format did not suit my work. The lack of depth of the telephoto lens as well as its bulkiness made me abandon this equipment when it came to subsequent expeditions.

Most of the photographs in this book were taken with the following equipment:

Cameras Nikon F, Nikon FE2, Nikkormat FTW. Two motor drives for the Nikon FE2.

Lenses Auto-Nikor: 24 mm, 35 mm, 50 mm, 105 mm, Macro 135 mm, 200 mm and 300 mm. Novoflex: 400 mm, 600 mm.

Film I used Kodachrome 64 and 25, two types I have always found satisfactory. The only drawback I experienced was that their low speed was not ideally suited to photographing animals. However, I always preferred to wait and to use a telelens with a short focal length. The quality of the end result is much better.

Acknowledgements

I would like to thank all the people who helped me discover the Kalahari and who contributed to the making of this book.

My greatest thanks go to my wife Laure. Her devotion, her understanding, her organizational skills and her constant enthusiasm were of vital importance to my work. I also wish to thank Michel Faure, who accompanied me on two of the trips, and all those friends who helped me and whose assistance I value so highly; I hope they will forgive me for not mentioning them individually. I am grateful, too, to all those who work for the protection of the environment in Botswana: more specifically, the staff of the Department of Wildlife and National Parks and the rangers of the national parks and reserves. They will find in this book an indication of the extent of my respect for their work. Finally, I wish to express my thanks to my friends Dr Bosenberg and his wife. I could not attempt to evaluate all the help they so generously provided.

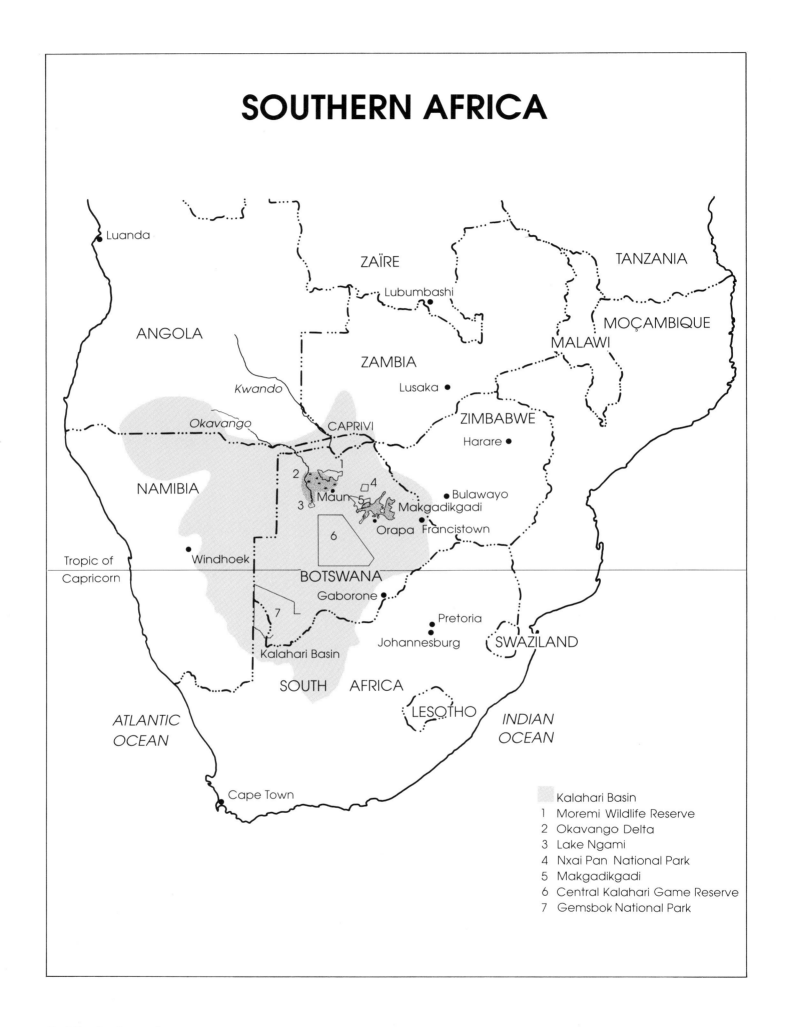

SOUTHERN AFRICA

• Luanda

ZAÏRE

TANZANIA

• Lubumbashi

ANGOLA

MOÇAMBIQUE

ZAMBIA

MALAWI

Kwando

Lusaka •

Okavango

CAPRIVI

ZIMBABWE

Harare •

1

2

4

NAMIBIA

• Maun

3

5

Makgadikgadi

• Bulawayo

6

Orapa • Francistown

Tropic of
Capricorn

• Windhoek

BOTSWANA

Gaborone •

7

• Pretoria

Kalahari Basin

Johannesburg •

SWAZILAND

SOUTH   AFRICA

*ATLANTIC
OCEAN*

LESOTHO

*INDIAN
OCEAN*

Cape Town •

Kalahari Basin
1 Moremi Wildlife Reserve
2 Okavango Delta
3 Lake Ngami
4 Nxai Pan National Park
5 Makgadikgadi
6 Central Kalahari Game Reserve
7 Gemsbok National Park

8 Kalahari

First encounter

Kalahari! The mere mention of the name of this lonely part of Africa often leads to confusion in people's minds. Some regard this vast region as being nothing more than a southern version of the Sahara. This would undoubtedly be a somewhat hasty judgement as, on the contrary, the Kalahari is a complex, abstract region which is, in many ways, difficult to define or understand. How, for example, can one conceive of a territory that has no natural or political borders and no proper biogeographical identity; a territory that remained, up until the end of the 19th century, virtually closed to explorers?

The vision that first greets visitors to the Kalahari is one of an utterly flat expanse dominated by a vast sky. However, the Kalahari consists of far more than merely earth and sky.

Firstly, it is one of the very few totally unsullied regions left on this earth; an enigma in a century committed to the wholesale desecration of precious natural resources. During my travels through the Kalahari, in the very heart of a region where the laws of nature still reign supreme, I once again came to understand the importance of such virgin territories, and the significance of the knowledge which they can impart to us.

The Kalahari is not a true desert in the normal sense of the word. The word 'desert' usually conjures up an image of a scarcity of water or, indeed, a total lack of it, and an absence of life-forms as a result. This is not the case in the Kalahari, which is actually a huge arid zone of the Sahel (arid savanna) type. With the exception of the Okavango Delta in the north, there are no permanent wetlands. For many months before the rejuvenating rains arrive, the soil remains parched and barren. As is the case in most arid regions of the planet, precipitation in the Kalahari is sporadic and unpredictable. Every year the rains are awaited with the same impatience by the animals as they are by the area's few human inhabitants.

For the people living on the edge of the Kalahari, the word *pula* means rain. In Setswana, *pula* also means 'luck'. Interestingly, the same word is given to Botswana's basic unit of currency. If a visitor were to give one of the local people a lift in his car, he would be well advised to use the word *pula* with circumspection, as this diversity of meanings frequently leads to misunderstandings!

In the Kalahari, water — whatever its source — is considered a vital and irreplaceable form of wealth for each individual. The Botswanan national motto is simply, 'Let there be rain!'

Water is so scarce in the central Kalahari that, apart from the Bushmen, no human being has managed to find a means to survive without bringing in extra supplies of the precious liquid. This is the reason why this region was never fully colonized, although Bechuanaland (as Botswana was then known) did become a British protectorate in 1884.

The dry areas of the Kalahari receive only some 200 to 500 millimetres of rain per year, compared, for example, with the South African Highveld, which receives about 600 to 800 millimetres annually. In Africa, only the Sahara and the Namib deserts receive less water than the Kalahari.

The long-awaited rains may arrive as early as September, although usually in November, and tend to flood a small area suddenly, leaving the rest of the Kalahari dry. Generally, the rainy season lasts until March, although its length does vary from year to year. Certain regions, such as the Okavango area, regularly receive a relatively large quantity of rain, whereas in other areas entire seasons can pass without a single drop of moisture falling.

In 1979, for example, the drought was so severe that some of the game herds were too weak to return to their grazing lands in the north. By the end of September that year, no rain had fallen over the Kalahari, except for certain isolated regions of the Okavango basin. People I met in Botswana showed me areas which had not received a solitary drop of rain for over seven years.

However, when the rains do come to the Kalahari, the storms are often sudden and violent, and one can easily find oneself stranded in deep mud. I experienced such a storm in 1985: clouds suddenly appeared over an empty horizon, and within minutes the sky had darkened. A few drops of rain fell, but at first I thought this was a false alarm. Then the skies suddenly opened, and the ensuing thunderstorm reached such massive proportions that I was forced to find a place where the soil would be firm enough to support the weight of my vehicle for at least three days. Astonishingly, the ground had been as hard as concrete only minutes before.

During the rainy months, such storms may occur several times a year, especially if it is a particularly wet season.

Although this type of sudden precipitation characterizes numerous African savannas, it is only in the Kalahari that one finds it impossible to predict whether a 'shower' which is a hundred metres away will drench one or whether it will simply dissipate. The swiftness with which these thunderstorms pass is another characteristic of this area: often a storm will last a few brief minutes and then the enormous cumulonimbus clouds vanish as if by magic, leaving a sky that is clear and blue to the horizon.

In spite of its unpredictability, the rainy season has its advantages for the fauna of the Kalahari and also for its human inhabitants, who must tolerate temperatures that can, exceptionally, reach over 42°C in the shade. Paradoxically, it is during the wet months of the year that the thermometers register the highest figures. For photographers like myself, the rainy season is the preferred time to visit the Kalahari because it offers not only spectacular views but also clean, crystal-clear air.

As I mentioned earlier, the central Kalahari does not have any permanent water-holes or perennial rivers, with the exception, of course, of the Okavango Delta and Lake Ngami. However, the rains that fall during the rainy season are often retained in the famous pans and in numerous natural depressions. Watering places are created when game herds trample the ground around these depressions, enlarging them and at the same time making the ground more impermeable. During a good year, some of these pans will retain water for up to six months.

In addition to these natural depressions, a few rivers cross the Kalahari. Actually, it is somewhat misleading to refer to them as 'rivers', as the water flows only sporadically. The Nossob River, for example, in the south of Botswana, flows on average only once every ten years.

One cannot overemphasize the importance of the water-holes and small freshwater pans. These are the places towards which all life converges, and it was alongside these pools that I had my most thrilling encounters with the wildlife of the Kalahari.

The extreme weather conditions of the Kalahari and its shortage of water have not to any degree inhibited the development of varied vegetation. The central Kalahari is characterized by thorn bushes, grasses and a few scattered trees. In some places the trees are somewhat more abundant than in others and they cluster together to form small thickets, which are greatly appreciated by the lions for the shade and shelter they provide. Most of the big trees are camel-thorn acacias and, of course, baobabs. These giants are well known by the Bushmen of the Kalahari — and by other travellers — who have, for centuries, used them as landmarks in an otherwise flat landscape. There is one baobab situated halfway between Nata and Maun which is so enormous that it can be seen from two kilometres away. It is difficult to believe that such a gigantic tree can derive sufficient moisture and nutrients from a barren soil that remains as dry as a bone for the greater part of the year. To my mind, this is one of the most astonishing feats of natural adaptation to an arid environment that I have ever encountered.

In the middle of the 19th century, the famous painter and explorer, Thomas Baines, was left speechless at the sight of a magnificent cluster of baobabs, and he subsequently painted several pictures of the group. The same trees that Thomas Baines so admired in 1862 still exist, and are to be found at Kudiakam Pan, south of the Nxai Pan National Park in Botswana.

From a biogeographical point of view, the Kalahari begins in the northern Cape, stretches over the whole of Botswana and extends right up into Angola. The vegetation of this vast territory (which covers more than a million square kilometres) comprises mostly those species adapted to arid conditions, although there certainly are areas of contrasting scenery. Some regions are totally devoid of vegetation, for example, because of the high salt content of the soil, whereas other areas are characterized by lush green oases teeming with species that bear little resemblance to those found in the drier parts of the Kalahari. All these diverse regions form one vast interdependent complex.

In a purely geographical sense, the Kalahari consists of a vast, shallow depression situated under the twentieth parallel and crossed by the Tropic of Capricorn. This depression is surrounded by the high plateaux of Zimbabwe in the north-east, the extreme western Transvaal and northern Cape in the south-east, and by the highlands of Damaraland (Namibia) in the west. The Kalahari was once a large internal sea, situated in a basin during the Archaean Era. The whole region is essentially a flat landscape; the plateau of fine sand which constitutes the Kalahari is broken only by a few topographical irregularities such as the Okavango basin and a number of granite outcrops. The altitude of the region is approximately a thousand metres. There are no real mountains; only a few scattered hills break the monotony of the landscape.

As I mentioned in the foreword, the Kalahari has to some extent been forgotten by the rest of the world. Even today, certain zones in central Botswana appear as if they have never been visited by man; it is true that only the Bushmen are capable of surviving there.

A section of the central Kalahari forms one of the biggest nature reserves in Africa, the Central Kalahari Game Reserve, which comprises some 51 800 square kilometres of land. No proper roads cross this virgin territory, which itself is surrounded on all sides by thousands of square kilometres of empty and unspoilt wilderness.

Before the middle of the 19th century, no white man had crossed the Kalahari. The first European to venture into the deepest heart of Bechuanaland, as Botswana was then called, was David Livingstone, the famous Scottish missionary and explorer, who travelled 1 100 kilometres across the Kalahari in an ox-wagon in 1842. Paradoxically, the neighbouring lands on the coasts of southern Africa had been colonized by the Boers, the British and the Portuguese long before the coming of David Livingstone. Livingstone was convinced that the extreme aridity of the Kalahari would prevent him from establishing a mission station there. Another missionary, his father-in-law, Robert Moffat, told Livingstone that in the northern parts of the region the land was greener and more densely inhabited; Moffat had, on an earlier expedition, seen the smoke from 'a thousand villages' rising above the vast plains. Unfortunately, he had not been able to investigate further, because to do so he would have had to cross the desolate wasteland of the Kalahari. Undaunted by this prospect, Livingstone, together with William Cotton Oswell and Mungo Murray, set off for the north again in June 1849. In August that year, their courage and audacity were rewarded when they discovered Lake Ngami, the home of hundreds of thousands of pelicans, flamingos and other water-birds.

After Livingstone, the Kalahari was traversed only by the occasional intrepid explorer. The first white man to set eyes on the Okavango River was Charles John Andersson, a Swede, in 1853. Later, an American G.A. Farini (born William Leonard Hunt) claimed to have discovered 'a long line of stone which looked like the Chinese Wall after an earthquake'. However, a few decades later, this discovery was proved to be but a figment of his imagination — on investigation not a single trace of this 'wall' was to be found.

During the last century, no serious exploration of the Kalahari was undertaken. One can understand, then, why the Kalahari — and specifically its central regions — has remained virtually unknown until quite recently. Unfortunately, this immense land now attracts all types of prospectors. Research into the region's mineral resources began in the seventies, and today there are large diamond mines at Orapa in the very heart of the Kalahari, and soda is soon to be exploited at Sowa Pan. This increase in mining operations, together with the inexorable expansion in numbers of domestic livestock and the building of numerous veterinary cordon fences, has had a noticeable impact on the environment. While this progress constitutes an undeniable success in terms of the economic and social development of the region, it leaves the worst to be feared in terms of the ecology.

The next decade will tell us if this, one of the last virgin wildernesses of southern Africa, will survive unspoilt into the centuries to come.

Wildlife in central Kalahari

An old Botswanan legend, passed on verbally from generation to generation, tells of how the Kalahari became so arid. Long ago, there was a huge marsh in which frogs were breeding prolifically. Because the frogs were polluting the water, the Bushmen started to kill them. Unfortunately, they did not know that these amphibians had magical powers which they used to prevent the water from evaporating. Every time a frog was killed, a little more water disappeared from the marsh. The Bushmen killed so many frogs that before long most of the water had evaporated and two-thirds of the Kalahari had dried out.

At the same time, the people who lived near Lake Ngami were experiencing a severe drought. Gradually most of the water evaporated and all of the fish in the lake vanished. Desperate, they decided that they would have to go to the marsh and try to catch some fish there. To their astonishment, they caught only frogs in their nets. They took hundreds of the frogs back with them to Lake Ngami but soon realized that they could not eat their catch. So they threw the frogs into the lake and, in a flash, the waters of the lake reappeared, and so did all the fish. This, according to legend, is how the Kalahari became a huge, dry savanna and how Lake Ngami remained full of water.

Like all legends, this story has some truth in it. Thousands and thousands of years ago, this vast semi-desert was a gigantic lake. Until fairly recently, in geological terms, water from the rivers of the region poured into the enormous pans of Makgadikgadi and Nxai, filling them to the brim. Where there is water, there is life, and life certainly flourished in the Kalahari. As the great pans slowly began to dry out, the animal life began to adapt itself to its new and hostile environment. This process took place over many thousands of years.

Many zoological groups are represented in this vast natural reservoir of fauna. Contrary to the legend I have just related, there are even a few species of frog that have managed to adapt to the harsh conditions of the savanna. Indeed, the drier regions of the Kalahari are the home of a curious frog which is capable of remaining buried under the sand for more than nine months of the year. The bullfrog *Pyxicephalus adspersus* emerges from the sand only during the short rainy season so that it may feed — and breed — at the rapidly filling pans and water-holes. This amphibian (which is widespread in sub-Saharan Africa) can grow to a length of twenty centimetres, not including the legs, and can weigh up to 1,2 kilograms. In 1986, I was lucky enough to discover one such specimen. Unfortunately this encounter proved fatal for the poor frog, who died under the wheels of my car while attempting to cross the track along which I was driving. I admit that I still feel guilty about having killed this poor fellow who, after having spent months buried beneath the hot sands of the Kalahari, was probably on his way to one of the rare water-holes or pans to find a mate.

As the central Kalahari is far more arid than the Okavango area, one does not usually encounter elephants or hippopotamuses there. There are exceptions, however. In 1986, my friend Dr Bosenberg told me how an elephant had caused panic by entering the Orapa mining development, which is more than 200 kilometres away from the animal's normal stamping grounds. Now and then, elephants are seen near the Nxai Pan, but an incident like this one is nevertheless rare.

Most animals typical of southern African savannas are to be found in the central Kalahari. Of all the hoofed animals, the graceful springbok *Antidorcas marsupialis* is perhaps the most enchanting. These gregarious animals are the fastest antelopes in the Kalahari: in fact, they can jump up to three metres in the air, their backs arched and their legs outstretched. For this reason, few predators succeed in getting close to them unless, of course, they happen to take them by surprise. Only the cheetah, another predator of the Kalahari, will directly pursue a springbok with any chance of success. The springbok have been widely hunted in the Kalahari by settlers, just as they have in other parts of southern Africa —and specifically South Africa, where entire populations were exterminated. I have heard people tell of the enormous herds that were encountered in the Kalahari during the last century, some of which are believed to have comprised 500 000 head of springbok.

The giraffe, kudu, gemsbok, eland, wildebeest and zebra which roam this wilderness are hunted by all the well-known predators of Africa: lion, cheetah, leopard, hyaena and wild dog.

Of all the animals in the Kalahari, Burchell's zebra *Equus burchellii* make up the largest segment of the mammalian biomass. I have often wondered how these animals, which always look well-fed and sleek, manage to derive sufficient nutrients from their meagre diet of grass. This question was foremost in my mind the day I encountered a large herd of zebra — probably 500 animals — roaming across a surface of parched, cracked mud where not a blade of grass was to be seen. However, it is a mistake to assume that Kalahari zebra lead a comfortable existence: every year, thousands of them die of thirst between Ghanzi and Orapa. In 1986, I personally witnessed this devastating phenomenon when I saw dozens of zebra carcasses piled up, ready for burning.

Zebras can easily satisfy their nutritional needs with meagre amounts of food — at least for a few days, that is — but water they cannot do without. For this reason they are forever on the move, even during the rainy season, when the water-holes are often situated far away from the pasture lands. When the last water-holes dry up at the end of the rainy season, the grass thins out and shrivels, and this is when the zebras and wildebeest begin to migrate northwards. Because of the vastness of the Kalahari, the herds tend to spread out over a wide area and the annual migration is thus not quite as spectacular as that which occurs in the Serengeti in Tanzania. No formal census has been taken of the larger mammals of the Kalahari, so nobody really knows how many animals are involved in the annual migration. The animal population of the region is undoubtedly still high but, according to the experts, it is diminishing at a steady rate. The only precise figures that we have at our disposal are those that account for dead animals. During the years when the rains come late, these figures can be very high indeed. For example, in 1961 and 1964, 80 000 carcasses were discovered in the area between Kuki and Makalamabedi.

In the past, such carnage was impossible because the animals did not come into contact with human beings. Today, the Central Kalahari Game Reserve is partially separated from the north by huge fences which are impassable by large game. These fences were erected during the fifties when the veterinary authorities of Botswana realized the economic importance of the country's domestic livestock and decided to take steps to protect the herds from diseases spread by wild fauna, such as foot-and-mouth disease. Without such controls many important international markets, such as that of the European Community, would not buy meat from Botswana.

These fences, although aimed at protecting Botswana's natural resources, are a real calamity for the fauna of the Kalahari. Today, there are approximately 1 300 kilometres of game-fencing separating the central Kalahari from the north of the region. A further hundred kilometres of fencing is at present being erected. This, one of the largest and wildest nature areas in the world, is slowly being strangled by veterinary cordon fences. The authorities decided that all contact between wild fauna and domestic animals should be avoided, and for good reasons, but they unfortunately did not survey the problem thoroughly enough before erecting the fences, nor did they take into account the basic needs of the wild animals. Perhaps the saddest aspect of the situation is that these fences have

not actually succeeded in preventing epidemics amongst domestic stock, which occur regularly. Furthermore, it has never been conclusively established that foot-and-mouth disease is transmitted to domestic livestock by game. Generally speaking, the Botswanan authorities feel strongly about retaining these fences: although they are hardly efficient, they are nevertheless a symbol of economic growth.

But to return to the fauna of the region: it would be presumptuous of me, I know, to try and describe in detail the wildlife of this region. The sheer diversity of the fauna makes this an impossible task, especially within the confines of a book of this size. For example, the Kalahari is home to over a hundred species of mammal, about thirty of which are carnivorous. I missed seeing more than half of these species, and, of those that I did see, I was able to photograph only a few.

In recent years much research has been carried out on the fauna of the Kalahari. The South African biologist Michael Mills and the Americans Mark and Delia Owens, for example, have made some very significant discoveries about the secretive brown hyaena *Hyaena brunnea*. Another biologist, F. Petter, of the Paris Museum, described a new species of mouse from the Kalahari as recently as 1978, Setzer's pygmy mouse (*Mus setzeri*). Anyone who believes that Africa is overexplored and overresearched will agree that there is still a great deal to be learned!

I nearly forgot to mention the ostrich *Struthio camelus* which — forgive my comparison — is as inseparable from the Kalahari scenery as the Alps are from Swiss scenery. Wild ostriches are so common in this region that one is always slightly surprised to look up and find that there are none of these birds in the vicinity. Long ostrich necks poking out of the tall grass like so many telephone poles are an everyday sight. I remember one morning feeling mildly astonished to discover that these familiar elements of the landscape were missing. I am aware that such comments must sound absurd to anyone who has not roamed these distant plains. However, be assured that the sight of a Kalahari landscape without ostriches is almost like seeing Paris without the Eiffel Tower. Ostriches are a part of the Kalahari's identity. I must add that that very same evening I had the good fortune to watch one of the most beautiful sunsets I have ever seen, which I photographed with the ubiquitous ostriches in the foreground, who had by that time returned!

In spite of the great numbers of ostriches in the Kalahari, I never discovered any nests. I did, however, have plenty of opportunities to observe male and female birds with very young chicks. Like most young birds, ostrich chicks resemble little balls of fluff. The parents, who keep their little ones tucked between their legs, are ever vigilant, because just one lapse of attention could leave the chicks easy prey for jackals or cobras, both of which are common in this region. In spite of their protectiveness, however, they often lose chicks and it is perhaps to compensate for these losses that each female will sometimes lay up to eight eggs at a time in a communal nest with two or three other females to make a total clutch of about two dozen.

I can think of nothing more thrilling than, after a long and tiring day on the hot and bumpy tracks of the Kalahari, to focus one's binoculars on these large friendly birds and their progeny. One must, however, be prudent in one's approach, as is the case with all wild animals. It is best to keep one's distance with ostriches and not to attract undue attention, as they tend to be extremely aggressive if they feel that the safety of their chicks or eggs is threatened. I once heard of a Bushman who tried to snatch some ostrich chicks from a nest and was killed by a violent kick from a fully grown bird. Ostriches can grow to two metres in height and can weigh up to almost 160 kilograms.

I observed the greatest number of ostriches around the Makgadikgadi Pans and Nxai Pan. In fact, I often encountered up to 300 ostriches in one day, which is considerably more than you would find in other parts of the Kalahari.

The ostriches enjoy the driest areas of the Kalahari and lead a nomadic life. Drought does not seem to affect them, nor does it prevent them from wandering up to ten kilometres away from the water-holes. However, when the opportunity arises, they drink as much as they can at one time.

Of all the birds indigenous to this region, the various bustards particularly attracted my attention. The Kalahari has five species, three of which are relatively common. These birds are to be found mainly on the open grassy and scrub plains and in the semi-desert areas. In size they vary from that of a big hen to that of a big turkey — indeed the kori bustard is reckoned to be the world's largest flying bird. Endowed with strong legs that are well adapted to walking long distances, bustards are forever striding around their territories looking for food. They eat mainly insects but also feed on lizards, small rodents, grass seeds and flowers.

The various species of Kalahari bustards, unlike the two European species, rarely live in groups but are to be observed dispersed on the savannas alone or in pairs. There are such large numbers of bustards in the Kalahari that, like the ostriches, it seems unthinkable that a day could go by without one observing them. On the vehicle tracks, where they usually congregate, these birds often forced me to brake suddenly, either because they dived out in front of the vehicle or because I simply wanted to stop and watch them. On one occasion, our luggage and equipment were thrown into total disarray when we came to a screeching halt in front of a red-crested bustard (or korhaan as it is called in South Africa) *Eupodotis ruficrista*.

The bustards are very pretty birds, especially the males, which show sumptuous plumage during their breeding displays. During my various wanderings in the Kalahari I had numerous opportunities to admire the feathers of the black bustard (or black korhaan) *Eupodotis afra*, a small bustard that is usually encountered on grassy plains dotted with thorn bushes. The male's upperparts are barred in black and gold, and its black breast and neck are separated by a bold white collar. Its legs are yellow, and its beak orange-red to bright carmine — a true work of art by Mother Nature. The female is more inconspicuous with buff not black on its neck and back.

Another species that deserves a special mention is the kori bustard *Ardeotis kori*, which has the curious habit of graciously offering its back as a perch to the carmine bee-eater *Merops nubicoides* in the north of the Kalahari where the ranges of the two species overlap. A small group of carmine bee-eaters will begin to flutter around a huge kori bustard, and then suddenly one, two or even three of these little hunters will dart up and perch casually on the back of the great bird. As it strides through the high grasses, the kori bustard inevitably disturbs numerous insects and the carmine bee-eaters swoop off their mobile perch to devour their prey. One can easily see the advantages the bustards bring to the bee-eaters, but it is a one-sided form of symbiosis for the bustards appear to gain nothing from the bee-eaters.

Should any reader decide to go to the Kalahari, I would advise him not to forget binoculars. Once you are there, you will be able to observe many fascinating bird species such as sandgrouse, coursers, shrikes, cuckoos, and over fifty species of birds of prey.

It is impossible for me to make a full list of all the animal species that I was able to observe on my three trips to the Kalahari. It is not for any lack of notes, but simply because such a list would be tiring for those who do not have the naturalist's inclination to observe and classify.

The fauna of the Kalahari is so vast that it is difficult to do justice to it in a book of this size. The animal species are innumerable and I have only observed a small number of them. These, then, are the reasons why I can only offer a few modest pictures and relate a few of my most thrilling encounters with the fauna of the Kalahari.

Birds of prey and scavengers

By the end of the morning on the plains, the suffocating heat has trapped the larger wildlife of the Kalahari, immobile, under the sparse available cover. Nothing stirs in the grasses, which slowly turn yellow in the burning sun. The horizon trembles in the torrid heat and the sky drowns along a blurred line. The glare prevents the use of binoculars, especially when they are adjusted to their maximum range.

For the big herbivores, and for the predators, it is siesta time. Their breathing slows, and the tension of the morning gradually eases. Surprisingly, the lion can be seen dozing alongside its favourite prey, the zebra and the gemsbok. The lion's aggression, however, is only temporarily suspended, and neither of these natural enemies would consider closing the tolerant distance that separates them. The truce will end as the afternoon draws to a close, at dusk. These, Nature's unbreakable laws, give each animal time to accumulate the energy necessary for survival.

Meanwhile, great gliders circle in the shining azure sky. The vultures are the only creatures of the Kalahari that take advantage of the oppressive heat, using the thermals with subtle mastery. They can glide for hours and over many kilometres without so much as flapping a wing.

Today, the 'dustmen of the sky' seem to be showing off — but the aim of their exhibition is to pinpoint food sources. Aware of their intention, Laure and I decide to follow them, first through the binoculars and then in our vehicle. Slowly, the great birds of prey move to the left, not far from a small group of acacias. This enables us to mark their position, and we travel towards them along an uncertain and indistinctly marked track.

Eight minutes have passed since they first appeared. The original twelve birds have now become twenty, circling above our heads without pause. Other vultures arrive, seemingly from nowhere, and join this ballet in the sky. Soon we will once again have to move without really knowing where this chase will lead us. An hour later, as the sun reaches its zenith, one of the vultures folds its wings and nosedives. A second one follows, and then a whole squadron. Their actions are, without doubt, quite deliberate. Vultures very rarely alight in the middle of the savanna for no reason: the effort required for these birds (which can weigh more than seven kilograms) to land and take off again constitutes a great expenditure of energy. There, somewhere behind that mound, probably lies a carcass.

In order not to disturb the vultures, we go around the mound and stop at a respectable distance. Sure enough, a wildebeest is lying on the ground, its abdomen ripped open. The kill must have occurred either last night or early this morning: the wildebeest has been only partly eaten and, in spite of the flies swarming into the open chest cavity, the flesh still seems quite fresh. A few metres from the carcass, the perpetrator of the kill, a lioness, warily watches these intruders who have fallen from the sky.

The vultures have now gathered in a close-knit group. Their patience is equalled by that of the lioness: each observes the other, until the undercurrent of animosity from the vultures seems to annoy the lioness, which becomes agitated. Not a single bird ventures nearer to the carcass, for the cat would certainly kill the intruder with a blow from its paw. If the lioness is full and game is plentiful in the area, she will abandon the remains of the prey. If not, the vultures will have to wait for hours, maybe days, for their share of the kill. But these birds can survive for several days on an empty stomach.

We have to show the same patience as the vultures, and wait. Fortunately, our vigil does not last more than an hour, as the fiery sun finally forces the lioness to seek the shade of a tree. The collective assault on the carcass begins immediately. The scavengers throw themselves eagerly at the gaping hole in the wildebeest's abdomen, but the opening is too narrow for all of them. Fights break out, and there is much wing-flapping; the kill becomes a mess. At times, we feel it is rather like watching a rugby match.

I have often observed animals feeding at kills, but I have never seen one like this in Africa. Usually, an established hierarchical order is adhered to at a carcass, with the immature and inexperienced birds giving precedence to the adults. In the general confusion this is not always evident, but each bird usually manages to get a part of the loot. Today, however, there are so many vultures that a scramble starts: a vulture leaves the scrum with a piece of meat, and is rushed at by half a dozen others. Clucking and furious cries can be heard as it tries in vain to defend its takings. Quickly, another band gathers at the carcass, while other vultures join the feast from the air. Soon it becomes impossible for us to distinguish the carcass; it has disappeared completely under a mass of moving wings and ruffled feathers.

Suddenly, three big birds of prey join the mêlée. They are lappet-faced vultures *Torgos tracheliotis*, the most impressive birds of the Kalahari, perhaps of all Africa. They are at least a quarter as big again as the other scavengers. Very soon they have appropriated the carcass. No blood is shed, there is no arguing; the others simply give way to the kings. Now and again a lappet-faced vulture spreads its gigantic wings and ruffles up its feathers to frighten the onlookers and to warn away the occasional troublemaker. This is classic vulture behaviour, and indeed is found in most living species: the establishment of a hierarchy of strength, respected by all.

Fifteen minutes later, the lappet-faced vultures begin to leave the carcass. They have gulped such a quantity of meat that their crops are swollen. After their departure, chaos reigns anew. In less than an hour the carcass will have been picked absolutely clean.

During my three expeditions in the Kalahari, I was able to experience scenes like the one described above only because of my vehicle. Without this means of overcoming the traveller's main obstacle — the road — many of my discoveries and observations would not have been possible. In the old days, explorers had to make do with archaic means of transport, such as ox-wagons, in areas where walking was impossible. It is perhaps for this reason that many aspects of life in the Kalahari have only come to light relatively recently.

It was from my four-wheel-drive vehicle that I photographed most of the scavengers and predators of the Kalahari, although this was not always ideal; I would have liked to observe the animals more discreetly. For a naturalist in Europe it would be unthinkable — and simply impossible — to operate as I did in Africa. In the Kalahari, however, the environmental impact of a metal body is hardly perceptible for the simple reason that one is alone, many kilometres from even a small village or any other form of human habitation. That is not all: a motorized vehicle is also a mobile asset, sometimes very useful, and always indispensable if one wants to study lions.

In my opinion, lions might well be the African predators one should fear most. Accidents as a result of confrontations with lions are reported every year. In Kenya, I narrowly escaped an attack by an old lion, and then only thanks to my car. My friend, Jean Michel Roggo, who was with me, came very close to witnessing a blood-letting that would definitely have prevented me from writing these lines.

But let us return to the 'dustmen of the sky'. For a long time I have felt a genuine admiration for these birds of prey. They are the last link in a food chain that incorporates an astonishingly large number of species. Although people feel repulsion at the sight of a vulture on a kill, I must admit that I do not.

Vultures feed almost exclusively on carrion, and although they can kill for themselves, they seldom do. As well as being useful links in the food-chain, these birds can be helpful in illustrating to the naturalist certain interesting aspects of biology. Think how lucky I was in the Kalahari to be able to see and photograph, in exceptional conditions, half a dozen different species! When one has spent a few moments with vultures, one starts looking at them differently. I have come to regard vultures as friendly — and even elegant — creatures.

The lappet-faced vulture *Torgos tracheliotus*, common in the Kalahari, is an impressive-looking bird with a breast marked with small black and white flecks. But the most surprising feature of this vulture is its expression, which seems to convey so much more than any other bird of prey. Look at its eyes — don't you think they look human? Even the ancient Egyptians regarded the vulture as the symbol of parental love. How I wish I could convince people of their beauty!

Vultures are equally remarkable in flight. Their wings, at once rigid and supple, are especially adapted to enable the birds to move with precision; their manoeuvres are executed absolutely perfectly. To save energy, vultures glide, remaining in the air for hours at a time, and even rising in the sky without so much as a flap of their wings. To enable them to achieve this, their wing structure is far more complex than one could ever imagine.

These masters of flight use the 'free' energy of thermals — warm rising air currents — to better advantage than any other bird. In the Kalahari, atmospheric conditions seem to suit this type of flying perfectly. Indeed, this is the reason why one rarely sees birds flying early in the morning. Rising thermals occur towards the end of the morning when the air has been sufficiently warmed by the rays of the sun. For the first hours of the day, these birds of prey are usually seen together in groups, perched on the branches of the few big trees of the Kalahari, patiently waiting for the air to warm up.

The large number of vultures is an indication that many predators exist. The Kalahari and its bordering regions are still home to lion, cheetah, hyaenas and wild dogs — and even if one does not see them, they are still there; they always make their presence felt at night in the camp.

This paradise is under great pressure from hunters. Poaching and legalized hunting outside the protected areas have taken their toll on the fauna. Shocking though it may seem, trophy-hunters in the Kalahari actually outnumber those travellers who visit the area merely to observe the wildlife. While I am not against hunting, and have said so in the past, I am totally against unnecessary slaughter, and I believe that the ineffectual regulatory measures applied in this environment will upset the ecological balance for ever.

In Botswana, hunting is considered a 'sport'. This brutal behaviour on the part of the human species repulses me as much as the wars which have changed, and are changing, many regions of the globe. In Botswana about 600 lions are killed each year, and this figure excludes poached animals. Some will say these deaths have no noticeable effect on the population, and that one can still see these animals frequently. They are quite wrong. Various biologists in the central Kalahari and in the Serengeti have stressed in their studies the problems inherent in the removal of the male lion from a pride. When a lion is shot, his lionesses may remain barren for months, even after other males join the group. A new male will sometimes kill existing cubs in order to stimulate the female to come into oestrus. I do not draw these statements merely from my own observations, but from those biological studies which have brought to light the problems facing the survival of lions.

Fortunately, this species does not yet appear in the Red Data Book, a list of endangered species prepared by the International Union for Conservation of Nature and Natural Resources (I.U.C.N.) to assist in the protection of wildlife. But for how long?

The spotted hyaena *Crocuta crocuta*, a much-despised animal which actually has many admirable qualities in spite of its bad press, also deserves a few words. It is quite common in the Kalahari and, unlike its secretive cousin the brown hyaena, can frequently be observed. It is most likely to be seen at dusk, when it leaves its den to commence its night's hunting. If this scavenger-hunter has so few admirers, it is probably partly because of its call, which is gloomy indeed. On the many occasions I have heard the call of the spotted hyaena, which can easily encompass two octaves, I have started — not from fright, but with the marvel of hearing its voice, to my mind the most beautiful in the Kalahari.

I digress here to say that nature is an inexhaustible wealth of marvels. I believe that its observation should not be limited to only one of our senses. Aside from sight, the sounds and scents of the wild are perceptible signals, especially at night when we cannot rely on our eyes.

Each animal species displays certain behavioural characteristics. It is wise to learn these and to take them into account when observing the animal; in this way, you will not disturb the creature, nor will you endanger your own security.

After numerous stays in Africa, I have developed certain ideas about the personality of the spotted hyaena. Even if it means shaking some well-known theories, I would venture to state that this hunter-scavenger is not as dangerous to man as we have been led to believe. In fact, I think that it is generally very wary of man. Not once has its behaviour led me to believe that it could represent a real danger.

I recall having been disturbed one evening by a beautiful hyaena which, probably hoping to find food, seemed determined to inspect every object we had in our camp. To chase her off we had only to make the noises one would usually make to scare off a dog or a cat. However, as soon as we had turned our backs, the thief crept back to the camp. This behaviour is not exceptional: Bernhard Grzimek has recorded spotted hyaenas devouring such objects as old brooms, shoes, bicycle saddles and old belts.

I was able to see for myself how sharp the teeth of this animal actually are when I found an aluminium bowl which had been totally shredded. It must not be forgotten, however, that numerous authors have related how careless travellers have been brutally mutilated, and even killed, by spotted hyaenas, while sleeping in the open at night.

In the Kalahari, the spotted hyaena seems to rely on the lion as its main provider of carcasses, although it is quite capable of hunting its own prey and can kill an animal the size of a zebra. In South Africa, hyaenas are known to feed on prey they have killed themselves, but in the Kalahari this would appear to be much rarer.

Although there is no predatory mammal endemic to (that is, confined to) the Kalahari — the brown hyaena, for instance, which is often associated with the Kalahari, is also found in Namibia right up to the shores of the Atlantic Ocean — certain carnivorous animals have definitely adapted themselves to this arid region. In the Kalahari, the lion seems able to go without water for lengthy periods without suffering any ill effects. Lions have even been seen eating tsama melons, better known as Bushmen's melons, which have a water content of ninety per cent. This astonishing observation throws into doubt those theories that claim that the lion cannot survive without water and that it has to drink deeply once it has eaten.

In the light of so many fascinating discoveries, I fail to understand the reason why human beings seem bent on the extermination of these magnificent animals. What pleasure is there in taking back to Europe a trophy which will tell us nothing about the Kalahari? After three expeditions I am still far from unravelling for myself all the secrets of this sanctuary of nature. I have missed seeing many species, such as the brown hyaena and the aardwolf *Proteles cristatus*, secretive animals that can be occasionally encountered, but which I have never been fortunate enough to observe.

The pans

Before I discuss the huge green paradise that is the Okavango Delta, I must first mention the great salty expanses of the Kalahari. David Livingstone, thought to be the first European to discover the Makgadikgadi Pans, described the pans as `reservoirs of rain water'. The saltiest pans, he added, were the 'Nchokotsa' and the 'Ntowenone' — we assume he was referring to the Sowa Pan and the Ntwetwe Pan. To Livingstone's disappointment, these pans did not produce fresh water, as he had hoped, but only salty brine. He went on to report that the first pan, with a circumference of thirty-two kilometres, was surrounded by mopane or *Bauhinia* trees. The second one, Ntwetwe, situated on a flatter area covered with soft fine grass, measured approximately twenty-four kilometres by a hundred and sixty kilometres. Livingstone commented that this pan was so large and flat that 'the latitude might have been taken on its horizon as well as upon the sea'.

The salt-pans are the remains of ancient lakes. Over the years they became covered in silt, which was carried onto the pans by the rivers which long ago crossed the Kalahari. Because these lakes became land-locked through geological faulting, there was no outlet for the water and it gradually began to stagnate, the increasing salt content slowly killing off the surrounding vegetation. Today, these perennial waters have disappeared altogether and it is only occasionally that rainwater fills the pans.

Vegetation on the pans is virtually non-existent. There are a few grasses and scattered bushes in areas where the salt content is at its lowest. The soil is constantly eroded by the wind and the calcrete substrate that is formed prevents the growth of vegetation. The dust of the pans is sometimes whirled into the air by the wind, forming curious little patterns in the sky. These 'genies' or 'dust devils' as they are called, are typical of the desert areas around the pans, but it is advisable to keep your distance from them as they can be dangerous.

The centre of the pan is accessible only in dry weather, provided that you have a suitable vehicle that is equipped with tyres that are able to grip the hard substrate beneath the light layers of fine dust. Crossing the pans in a vehicle is an interesting experience but one inevitably has to spend hours cleaning dust out of the engine and the air filter afterwards. It is not advisable to attempt to cross these pans when it is raining, because it is very easy to get stuck in the mud of the Makgadikgadi plains. These areas are very isolated and a visitor whose vehicle gets bogged down in the mud is truly at the mercy of the harsh elements.

The pans, which are of various sizes, are found in great numbers virtually everywhere in the semi-desert regions of the Kalahari. During the rainy season, the sky often fills with small, uniformly shaped cumulus clouds, creating one of the most spectacular sights of the Kalahari.

A few kilometres away from these strange wastelands, one once again encounters the fine, soft grass described by Livingstone, although in this region it is relieved by clusters of lala palms *Hyphaene petersiana*. This tree, which is generally rare, is the second tallest species of tree in the Kalahari; the tallest is, of course, the baobab.

If one observes the grassy plains carefully, one will notice dozens and dozens of small paths, the tracks made by great herds of wildebeest, zebra and other hoofed animals. During the rainy season these herbivorous animals assemble in these areas because they offer not only attractive pastures but also the opportunity of obtaining water and essential salty deposits.

When travelling from Gweta in the north of Makgadikgadi to Mopipi in the south, one inevitably has to cross Ntwetwe Pan, unless, of course, one has lost the way. The track is no more than a path and is barely visible in places. On this flat area, where not a blade of grass is to be seen, one can observe thousands of springbok, the delicate gazelles of southern Africa. Extremely well adapted to the harsh conditions of these areas, the springbok are able to roam over hundreds of square kilometres of utterly deserted wilderness without suffering any adverse effects from the hostile conditions and the merciless sun of the Kalahari. This is not the case with the zebra and wildebeest, which will cross the pans only if forced to do so, and then in the quickest possible way. One can see these herds from hundreds of metres away as their hooves stir up clouds of fine dust. The flat areas of the pans are certainly a curiosity for the visitor, although, admittedly, the fauna is not as diverse as it is in the neighbouring areas where the vegetation offers abundant food and shelter for numerous species of animal.

During my various travels I used a bivouac a few kilometres away from Gweta, in an area where the acacias and lala palms offered welcome shade and leafy greenery. As it was not far from the Makgadikgadi Pans, we nicknamed this small paradise 'the Makgadikgadi camp-site'. There we observed many of the species that are to be found in the Kalahari.

One of these was the gemsbok *Oryx gazella*, that splendid antelope with its long, almost straight, rapier-sharp horns. Gemsbok are scarce elsewhere in this region and are not often observed.

From our hide-out we were also able to watch many of the small mammals that inhabit this arid environment, sometimes in surprisingly large numbers. In my experience, these small animals rarely interest those travellers who come to Africa intent only on seeing 'big game'. We saw some bat-eared foxes, those curious creatures with disproportionately large pointed ears, as well as dwarf mongooses, suricates and ground squirrels. From dawn to dust, the Kalahari teems with life, proving once again that the region is not a true desert.

In 1985, I observed a whole series of burrows just a few kilometres away from our camp-site. These were occupied by dozens of ground squirrels and by a few dwarf mongooses. They all seemed to be living in perfect harmony, sometimes even sharing the burrows. Every time we came close, the whole lot of them would disappear in a flash, only to reappear a few minutes later. After a while, the animals became used to our presence and we were able to examine them at our leisure.

I also encountered an Egyptian cobra *Naja haje annulifera* there. It was a very beautiful reptile and, to my great surprise, it allowed me to photograph it from all angles, obligingly rearing up in a characteristically aggressive manner. At this stage, I would like to dispel the notion that Africa is full of snakes. Some people believe that only those who have the soul of a kamikaze pilot should visit certain parts of Africa! While it is true that there are many more snakes in Africa than there are in Europe, and that some are truly dangerous, one nevertheless encounters them very rarely. In the space of two months in 1985, I saw only three snakes, one of which was the cobra, the only snake I managed to capture on film for this book.

On most maps of Botswana — and there are few of them — the two big pans of Makgadikgadi are often represented as being permanently flooded. In reality, the flooding of Ntwetwe Pan and Sowa Pan has become more and more sporadic in the last few years because of the persistent drought. To fill Ntwetwe Pan now would take many weeks of heavy rainfall. The rain would first have to swell the Okavango River, which would then pour into the Boteti River and fill up Lake Xau, which itself has been dry for a few years. If there is still sufficient water left over, Ntwetwe will be flooded with water. Sowa Pan can be filled in the same way by the Nata River which is fed by good rains in western Zimbabwe. When this happens, millions of microscopic organisms encrusted in the dry mud will come to life, forming a planktonic 'soup' that attracts numerous flamingos, normally inhabitants of Lake Ngami and the Mopipi Dam.

At present, the pan region consists of two protected zones: Makgadikgadi Pans Game Reserve and Nxai Pan National Park. Half-way between Nata and Maun, they cover 4 144 and 2 590 square kilometres respectively. The Makgadikgadi and Nxai Pans are almost unknown regions of the Kalahari, and fortunately there are still very few people who venture into these wild areas.

An oasis in the Kalahari

Slowly and silently, our small boat cleaves the calm, clear waters of the river. The rhythmical movements made by our guide as he 'poles' the craft through the water with a long stick do not compromise the stability of the fragile skiff that glides so smoothly; indeed, we are amazed at his control.

After the inferno of the land we can at last enjoy a well-deserved rest and can travel without having to listen to the diabolical noise of wheels drumming on corrugated earth. We are stunned by our surroundings: so much crystal-clear water and a landscape so green that we find it hard to believe that we are only a dozen kilometres away from the arid Kalahari bush. Generally, one navigates the Delta in *mekoro*, wooden dugouts. The canoe in which we are travelling is certainly not typical, but it enables us to navigate more safely and offers more room for our equipment than a *mokoro* does.

Standing up in the glass-fibre boat, my companion Michel Faure marvels, as I do, at the multitude of birds that watch us pass. Squacco herons display their delicately powdered coats, purple herons tuck their heads into their shoulders, and small green-backed herons thread their way nimbly through the papyrus if we pass too near them. Above our heads, flocks of pygmy geese cause the air to vibrate, and to our left a malachite kingfisher watches the water with a skilled eye. On the bank, perched on a huge sycamore fig, a splendid great white egret in an immaculate white coat pays scant attention to us as we pass just a few metres away. The dense riverine vegetation and tall papyrus prevent us from spotting mammals on the banks, but we do see an otter, as lithe as its European cousin. From time to time, we turn to look at the water, as clear as glass; our boatman, who is a crafty fisherman too, occasionally hooks one of the swiftly swimming fish out of the river.

The river widens into a small lagoon, then divides into several tributaries. Our guide, with the familiarity of one who has lived all his life in the swamps, chooses a right-hand turn. Further on, he takes an arm to the left and, still farther, one to the right. We meander through the Delta in this way until we finally return to our base camp, situated on an island edged with huge fig trees.

Our catch — half a dozen big tilapia and four tiger-fish — is eaten with pleasure under a sky glittering with thousands of stars, while in the distance the roars of a lion, in love or simply hungry, as we are, resound in the bush.

What more could we want?

If I had started this book by describing the Okavango, it is probable that no reader would have taken me seriously, knowing that the Kalahari and Botswana are situated in one of the driest areas of southern Africa. And yet the famous Okavango Delta is truly to be found in the heart of the Kalahari. This gigantic oasis is the green lung of the arid vastness of the tropical bush.

As I noted at the beginning of this book, the interdependence between these two wild sanctuaries is unquestionable. But what does this famous delta consist of, and how has it come to exist in a country scarred by dry river-beds?

The source of the Okavango lies many miles from the Delta itself, in the highlands of Angola, where it rises not far from the sources of the Zambezi and Kwando rivers. The Okavango crosses Angola, southbound, and when it reaches Cuangar, on the Namibian border, the topography of the continental plateau forces it to change its course drastically. A little further on, it crosses the Caprivi Strip to flow into Botswana's Ngami district. There, instead of joining the Zambezi and becoming a tributary, the Okavango reaches a system of tectonic faults which interrupt its flow, and so it pours out onto the yellow sands of the Kalahari to form a huge delta which spreads over more than 15 000 square kilometres.

Interestingly, there is evidence that at one time the Boro, one of the distributaries of the Okavango, joined the Kwando and, through it, the Zambezi. Nowadays the Boro leaves the Okavango a few kilometres away from Shakawe and runs parallel to the main river. At Xaa, the Boro runs east before disappearing underground. Its ancient bed is visible proof that in former times it fed directly into the Zambezi.

The Delta is situated at the southern extremity of the Great African Rift Valley. Earthquakes, even small ones, continually disturb the river-bed, at times altering the topography of some areas. The hydrological system of the region is very complex, and is further complicated during the dry season when, paradoxically, the Okavango is in flood because it is the dry season in Angola. All these factors make the river a real Chinese puzzle for casual observers.

Few people are fortunate enough to venture into the twisting tributaries of this gigantic swamp. To penetrate the depths of the Okavango Delta requires a means of transport other than a four-wheel-drive vehicle, because in one of these you would run the risk of hitting and injuring or killing the many animals that live on the river-banks. An aeroplane might be the best solution but you may well return home without having experienced the myriad sounds and scents of this paradise. Such a journey would truly be an illusion, for the Okavango guards its secrets jealously. This is a region of elephants, hippopotamuses and crocodiles — these animals are always present, but many impatient visitors return home disappointed at having seen only a few of them, or merely their tracks. Where the great savanna gives way to the tangled swamps with their luxuriant vegetation, wildlife becomes invisible.

The birds, however, always maintain a high profile, and their abundance in places is beyond the wildest imagination of the European ornithologist who has never been to Africa. In the Okavango Delta I counted no fewer than eight species of kingfisher; all in all, I saw about 320 species of birds, among which were the most remarkable and the most beautiful to be found in Africa.

Of course, the fauna can be just as plentiful in other regions of Africa, but here, in the heart of the Delta itself, man does not compete with wild animals for space. It is true, however, that he intrudes at times, as we did when we explored the area, or as the poachers do when they hunt crocodiles. The human population of the Delta is one of the lowest in the world: 2,5 people per 100 square kilometres as opposed to an average of 170 people per 100 square kilometres for the whole of Botswana. In comparison, France supports as many as 10 000 inhabitants per 100 square kilometres, Switzerland 15 000, and Belgium about 33 000.

The doorways to the Delta were probably first opened hundreds of thousands of years ago, by the Bushmen. Later came the baYei (a name which means 'from the east'), a descendant of whom might guide you through the waterways of the Okavango swamps today. The heart of the Delta was not explored by Europeans until the second half of the 19th century. 'Sleeping sickness' fever caused by the dreaded tsetse fly, and the dense vegetation of the Okavango's tributaries, proved barriers to exploration.

It was ivory, a coveted and precious material, that attracted the first settlers, even before David Livingstone's arrival. In his 1849 journal, Livingstone reported that a trader in his party was 'purchasing ivory at the rate of ten good large tusks for a musket worth thirteen shillings'. He went on to say, 'They were called "bones" and I myself saw eight instances in which the tusks had been left to rot with the other bones where the elephant fell ... in less than two years after our discovery, not a man of them could be found who was not keenly alive to the great value of the article.'

Less than fifteen years after Livingstone's arrival, the ivory 'mines' in the north of Bechuanaland had been shamelessly looted by a handful of hunting companies. During the year 1865 alone, these people killed 5 000 elephants; this figure does not include the animals shot by independent hunters. Business was booming, to the detriment of the wildlife. In the same year, also in Botswana, 3 000 leopards, 3 000 lions, 3 000 ostriches and some 3 500 other animals were massacred. Fortunately, the hunters experienced difficulties reaching the heart of the Delta and this slowed the killing frenzy, which could otherwise have been catastrophic. The result of such slaughter in the more densely populated South Africa, for example, is that today that country's wildlife — only a shadow of what it once was — is confined essentially to a handful of national parks and game reserves.

Nowadays the traveller can reach the furthest corners of the Delta more easily. Those who are lucky enough to explore one of the many tributaries of the Okavango are often struck by the feeling of permanence and tranquillity that prevails. The water runs calmly, without any turbulence, brushing past islands, sometimes fringed by luxurious vegetation where huge fig trees grow, or edged by sandy banks where majestic lala palms stand. Lagoons dappled with lotus flowers and other colourful waterlilies, hundreds of pools kept open by the hippopotamuses, impenetrable papyrus forests: this is the oasis that rests on a 300-metre-thick cushion of accumulated Kalahari sand.

Contrary to what one might expect, the water is surprisingly clear. Neither sediments nor dangerous pathogenic organisms are to be found in the pure waters of the river. One can drink this water without fear of contracting one of the diseases that normally proliferate in these latitudes. Some specialists actually consider the water of the Delta to be among the purest in the world. David Livingstone wrote of the

Thamalakane, `...we found (the water) to be so clear, cold, and soft, the higher we ascended, that the idea of melting snow was suggested to our minds.' It is true that one can clearly see small fish swimming as deep as five metres below the surface.

Leaving Maun, one of the few established settlements in the north of the country, one can travel north-east into one of the only territories that can be covered by vehicle. Beyond the tiny village of Shorobe, about forty kilometres from Maun, a sand track leads to a peninsula that juts into the Okavango Swamps. This is the Moremi Wildlife Reserve, named after Chief Moremi III, who donated the land for conservation purposes in 1963. Covering about a third of the Delta and populated by diverse wildlife, it is equipped with rudimentary facilities — fortunately — for the observation of indigenous and migratory animals.

Until 1986, the Moremi Wildlife Reserve was visited by only a few Botswanan citizens and by those tourists who felt confident that they would be satisfied with the meagre comforts of a bush camp. Although one should not expect fully equipped accommodation, tarred roads and supply stores, one must realize that one can see countless numbers of antelope, zebra, giraffe, buffalo and large predators — and, of course, the inevitable elephants which are such a menace on the weathered roads of this wild sanctuary. In the Moremi it is possible to see more than 500 elephants in a single day.

You should not visit the Moremi Wildlife Reserve without planning well in advance and taking the necessary precautions, otherwise you might well have similar problems to those my companion and I experienced in 1986.

As in all good adventure stories, we started out early in the morning that day, determined to reach a place that we particularly liked. After days of rationing our water, our main aim was to have a bath — in the clear waters of the Okavango, of course. The road, which we knew well, having used it several times, was flooded so we had difficulty in finding our bearings. Every few hundred metres, a small lagoon or mud puddle would slow our progress.

Finally, we found ourselves faced with a very daunting stretch of water. After lengthy deliberation, we tested the solidity of the ground several times and measured the depth of the water. We agreed to try to drive through it. I will skip the details, but suffice it to say that we ended up at a camp-site we had not set out to find. The whole operation caused us two and a half days' work under the car, as well as a delightful night with the usual welcoming committee of lions, elephants, hyaenas and, of course, mosquitoes. I still recall my friend's face as, at first light, he woke to find himself stranded on the top of a vehicle in a large pool of water.

This type of adventure is easily encountered if one strays from the well-trodden path. Fortunately, this one had a happy ending. Others are sometimes more tragic, as was the case reported by my friend, Dr Bosenberg, in 1985. Although I have always been a little sceptical when it comes to stories about man-eating lions, I changed my opinion after having heard what happened at Xakanaka, in a sector of the Moremi reserve near one of the tributaries of the Okavango.

One night a young girl was pulled from her open tent by a lion, a few metres from the place where Dr Bosenberg, his wife and his daughter had set up their camp. It was not the first time such an accident had occurred. The lions of Xakanaka are becoming more and more bold with campers. The girl's remains were never found. Such tragedies can be avoided if one sleeps inside a vehicle or in a closed tent. It is possible that this type of misadventure is occurring more frequently because of the great increase of tourist numbers — such travellers are often badly informed and are under the impression that they are staying in a reserve that is as safe as those found in South Africa.

Man is the only creature capable of changing the intrinsic character, the unspoilt beauty, of this incomparable environment. As long as it remains untouched, the Okavango and the great wild Kalahari will be more than just a remnant of past beauty, threatened with extinction.

Epilogue

Now we have reached the end of our journey, a trip which has taken us into some of the wildest areas of southern Africa. This tour was not, of course, a comprehensive one. Some readers may well reproach me for not having dealt with certain regions or aspects of the Kalahari, others will say that I dwelt too long on other topics. However, as I mentioned earlier, my aim was not to present a detailed view of the Kalahari. My words were those of a naturalist wishing to share his wonder and his joy at encountering the beauty of an unspoilt area of our planet.

In spite of its wildness and isolation, the sanctity of the Kalahari is threatened by progress. I believe that if steps are not taken within the next few years, this region will be systematically destroyed during the decades to come.

I hope that it will not be too long before people realize the threats facing the Kalahari. Remember that it is useless to protect a species if its habitat is destroyed. The bigger that habitat is, the better the chances of survival will be for those species which depend on it.

To understand this concept, one must examine what has happened in other areas. Take Europe, for example: certain areas of the continent have become inhospitable to animals, either because their natural environment has disappeared or because it has been altered in some way. When we notice that these animals are threatened with extinction, we invent what we consider to be ingenious solutions. Zoos, natural history museums and tiny, overpopulated reserves are all examples of these solutions. However noble our intentions, these solutions are far from perfect.

In Botswana it has not yet been considered necessary to take these steps. In many ways, I am optimistic that the vast wilderness that makes up the Kalahari will be saved. However, as I have already stressed elsewhere in the book, progress is already beginning to transform the region. New fences for controlling live-stock are planned, for example — the selfsame fences that have already caused the deaths of thousands of grazing antelope and zebra. There is also talk of new mining operations which will reach into the very heart of certain nature reserves.

In the past few years, there has also been an intensified battle against the tsetse fly, with the aim of protecting domestic animals from *nagana* and humans from trypanosomiasis or sleeping sickness. Moreover, certain areas along the Okavango seem to be attracting an increasing number of tourists and there has been talk of developing more sophisticated accommodation facilities.

Personally I am very unhappy about the prospect of increased promotion of tourism in the Okavango Delta. This type of development invariably has repercussions for the environment. The conventional tourist is very unlikely to be satisfied with the rough accommodation and harsh conditions that I have described and will demand fully-equipped camps, tarred roads, Western food and recreational areas, all of which make him feel secure while still allowing him to indulge his thirst for adventure and exotic venues. That is what is called progress.

I sincerely hope that the people of Botswana will follow a reasonable development policy which will protect the natural resources of the country and preserve them for future genera- tions. For a big country that is not threatened by overpopulation, this would hardly be a risky venture. If Botswana does not take steps to guard its riches, it could lose them for- ever. As an old Botswanan proverb says, *Tshwene ebonye mapalomo mafologo gaeabona:* 'See the baboon: he knows how to climb the tree but he doesn't really know how he is going to come down.'

Captions to the photographs

The Kalahari is not a true desert, but a huge arid savanna, similar to the Sahel region. Trees — such as these lala palms *Hyphaene petersiana* — break the flat line of the horizon.

This landscape near Mopipi, swept by the fine dust that blows off the Makgadikgadi Pans, resembles the Nigerian Sahel. Because of the harsh climatic conditions, the winds and the lack of humus in the soil, plant life is not all that diverse. Only species that have adapted to the arid conditions - such as acacia trees — can survive here.

Before the onset of the rainy season, heavy clouds may daily threaten the wild stretches of the Kalahari, which receive only some 200 to 500 millimetres of rain annually. The rains may be late and, in some years, whole areas remain dry. Usually the rainy season lasts from September to March, but in the Kalahari one cannot predict precise dates.

The central Kalahari during the rainy season: a barren plain dotted with clusters of low thorn bushes and scattered grasses. Soon, thousands of herbivores will cross these stretches of open savanna, playing their part in the maintenance of this environment. But their stay will only last a short season.

A localized thunderstorm has broken in the distance. This impressive formation of cumulonimbus clouds is typical of the Kalahari. In a short time, a clear blue sky will once again prevail, and only small parts of these huge expanses will have received rain. The following night new clouds may appear, but it is very unlikely that rain will fall again over the same area.

The rain has filled a depression, but the water will remain for only three or four weeks. With the exceptions of the Okavango Delta, there is no permanent water in the Kalahari. The parched soil must wait for many months for the onset of the rejuvenating rains.

Ntwetwe Pan, a dry reminder of what was once a prehistoric sea. The meagre offering of rain falling in the distance is not likely to fill it again.

The tawny eagle *Aquila rapax* is perhaps the commonest bird of prey of the Kalahari. Its speed and daring make it a dangerous predator. It is not uncommon to see it near seasonal water-holes.

It is near the great salt-pans that one can best appreciate the immensity of the wild plains of the Kalahari. No trees and no topographical landmarks break the monotony of the landscape. It is unwise to move away from the few roads that cross the region without taking a compass, as vehicle tracks can be wiped out by the wind within a few hours.

Some birds are well adapted to the harsh conditions of the Kalahari, their dun coloration blending with their surroundings. This Temminck's courser *Cursorius temminckii* would probably have escaped detection had it remained still as I approached.

After having crossed a huge zone covered with small, coarse grasses, we come upon Ntwetwe Pan. Man is not often seen here; his presence would be compromised in the long run because of the aridity of the land and the lack of fresh water.

A pair of yellow-throated sandgrouse *Pterocles gutturalis*. The sandgrouse is particularly well adapted to life in desert areas. However, it cannot live without drinking, and covers long distances each morning and night to quench its thirst. The flight direction of a sandgrouse in the Kalahari will often indicate the whereabouts of the nearest water.

David Livingstone is said to have been the first European to discover the Makgadikgadi Pans. In 1849 he described them as huge rainwater reservoirs; nowadays these stretches are very rarely covered with water.

A double-banded courser *Rhinoptilus africanus* sits on its eggs. Certain birds of the Kalahari do not nest in trees, but simply deposit their eggs on the ground. A scrape in the soil serves as a nest for this species.

Moving away from the Makgadikgadi Pans, sparse vegetation again makes an appearance. The rains, if they come, will transform the land into green pastures, and thousands of herbivores will return from the south to graze upon the tender grass. In this picture, the traces of their last migration can be seen.

The pale chanting goshawk *Melierax canorus* is a medium-sized bird of prey. It is a specialist hunter of birds, taking coursers, sandgrouse and the smaller passerines of the Kalahari, but also preys on lizards, snakes, insects and small mammals.

Ostriches dot the horizon between the lala palms. The sun is setting rapidly and the temperature has already dropped considerably. Night temperatures sometimes fall to freezing in the Kalahari.

One of the most typical scenes of the Kalahari: a grassy savanna dotted with acacias and other stunted thorn bushes. In spite of its arid appearance, abundant life exists on this plain. To discover it, and to understand why the Kalahari is not a desert, one has to travel into the very heart of this savanna.

Strange skies sometimes herald the end of the day. These magnificent gilt-edged clouds are not the forerunners of a storm, however; tomorrow morning they will have disappeared, to return again the following night. We are in the middle of the rainy season but no rain has fallen on the Makgadikgadi Pans for days.

One of the rarer reptiles I came across in the Kalahari. To my delight, this Egyptian cobra *Naja haje* allowed me to photograph it without it becoming too aggressive. It was a good size, like many of the cobras in this region, which can grow to as long as three metres.

In some regions of the Kalahari the carmine bee-eater *Merops nubicoides* hunts with the kori bustard *Ardeotis kori*. This is not, however, an example of true symbiosis: the stowaway is interested only in the grasshoppers its transporter disturbs while walking.

Great numbers of Burchell's zebra *Equus burchellii* roam the plains of the Kalahari; we do not know the exact figure but it must be in the region of several hundreds of thousands. Although they invariably appear well fed, very dry years can reduce their food supply — and therefore the population — considerably.

When there are no bustards available, any perch can be used as an observation post. The carmine bee-eater feeds only on insects: grasshoppers, bees and wasps are this charming little hunter's favourite foods.

Gemsbok *Oryx gazella*, along with springbok, are the most well-adapted herbivores of the Kalahari. These elegant antelope live in small groups in the most arid parts of the region where they are a favourite prey of lions.

Extremely well adapted to the Kalahari, the springbok *Antidorcas marsupialis* is found there in its thousands. Further south, in South Africa's Cape Province, its numbers were severely reduced in the last century but it is now a popular game-farming species.

One of the two flamingo species occurring in the Kalahari, the lesser flamingo *Phoenicopterus minor*, photographed on Lake Ngami. When the Makgadikgadi Pans are flooded, thousands of these birds converge there to feed on the plankton that flourish in the nutrient-rich waters.

The bat-eared fox *Otocyon megalotis* is one of the smallest members of the dog family in Africa. It is very common in the Kalahari. Several times I came across small groups hunting grasshoppers, one of their favourite meals

Bush thickets such as this one always lead to fascinating discoveries: often lions or spotted hyaenas come to look for a little shade, and tree-nesting birds may be found in the branches.

A yellow mongoose *Cynictis penicillata* in its grey phase typical of Kalahari populations of this species, hesitates for an instant before disappearing into the burrow of a ground squirrel. Mongooses are common on the African savannas and identifying them often presents problems, even to the specialist.

The white-backed vulture *Gyps africanus* commands attention at a kill. The presence of scavengers is always a sign of a healthy environment, and the Kalahari is home to several species.

A marabou stork *Leptoptilos crumeniferus* flies over Lake Ngami. This is the largest member of the stork family. Marabou storks are partly scavengers; I have seen them near the lake arriving in their thousands to feed on fish stranded on the banks.

The spotted hyaena *Crocuta crocuta* is another of the scavengers of the Kalahari. This fierce-looking female has her pup with her. As soon as they are old enough to participate in the hunt, the small hyaenas will follow the adults during their nocturnal rounds. However, it is not unusual to see them during the day too.

The lappet-faced vulture *Torgos tracheliotus* is the largest African vulture. Its wingspan may measure up to 2,7 metres, and with its powerful beak it is capable of tearing apart the strongest hide. Like most other vultures, it is not a predator, its food consisting mainly of carrion.

Nxai Pan is situated in the north-east of Botswana. It is covered with meagre scrub vegetation, and only a few groups of acacias break the monotony. Because the vegetation cover attracts many herbivores during the rainy season, the fauna of the Kalahari flourishes abundantly here.

In the Kalahari a carcass attracts much attention. Here a marabou stork *Leptoptilos crumeniferus* patiently waits its turn. In the lean season, vultures may wait for long periods at a time for their turn at a kill, but during the rainy season carcasses are plentiful.

In the arid regions of Makgadikgadi and Nxai, I came across numerous black korhaans (or bustards) *Eupodotis afra*. They advertise their presence by their raucous, squawking calls. The black korhaan seems to thrive far away from water.

A whole story could be written about this zebra carcass. When one crosses the Makgadikgadi plains, such sights are common.

The ornate head of this splendid gemsbok *Oryx gazella* cannot but remind one of a traditional African mask. Very often the striking markings on the faces or the rumps of these antelopes are used for identification purposes by researchers.

In the Kalahari, the ostrich *Struthio camelus* holds all records. It is the largest and fastest-running bird on earth. There are so many of them that at times the silhouettes of the birds become an integral part of the landscape. In this picture the male, dressed in black and white, protects the offspring of one of his females.

This lioness has just killed a gemsbok and hidden it under the tree where her cub is taking shelter. In a few months the cub will be big enough to go hunting with her.

Like all the great predators of the Kalahari, lions are active mainly during the night or at first light. Daytime is reserved for sleeping.

 The giant eagle owl *Bubo lacteus* is the largest nocturnal bird of prey found in the Kalahari. This strong predator favours semi-wooded savannas where acacias predominate. Its very characteristic hollow call betrays its presence.

 The lion *Panthera leo* is the largest representative of the cat family in Africa. In certain regions of the Kalahari they are still numerous, but more than 600 lions are shot senselessly every year. Although hunting is legal in some regions, it often affects populations near protected areas.

 A water-hole at night in the Moremi Wildlife Reserve. Surrounded by the arid immensity of the Kalahari is the world's largest oasis — the Okavango Delta.

 A cheetah *Acinonyx jubatus* in the shade of a termitarium. This beautiful creature — the fastest land mammal — is on the decline in the Kalahari, as is the case elsewhere in Africa. Although they are still plentiful on the Makgadikgadi and Nxai plains, these animals are rarely observed.

 The same water-hole in the morning. The African fish-eagle *Haliaeetus vocifer* can be seen as an environmental indicator: its presence tells of the proximity of permanent water or wetlands.

 The variety of birds of prey in the Kalahari is astonishing; ornithologists have recorded fifty-one in this region alone. More a scavenger than a hunter, the yellow-billed kite *Milvus migrans parasitus* is commonly seen. This individual was attracted by the remains of our meal and kept us company for more than two hours.

 The African fish-eagle can remain still for hours, contemplating its fishing beat. Its vigilance reflects its acute sense of territory; the only other member of its species it accepts is its mate, to whom it remains faithful for life. In the Okavango Delta it is a common bird of prey, if not an abundant one.

It is said that this baobab *Adansonia digitata* is the biggest in all Africa. At its base the evidence of passing elephants can be seen in the damaged bark, which they gouge out and chew in the dry season.

 The Okavango is a paradise for waders, particularly herons. Seventeen species of herons and their relatives are represented in this sanctuary of swamp ornithology. Here, a great white egret *Egretta alba* is taken by surprise while fishing from behind a curtain of rushes.

 The lilac-breasted roller *Coracias caudata* is common in the Okavango region. Tropical countries usually have a far more varied and colourful bird population than is found in temperate regions.

 Another example of one of the ornithological jewels of the Delta: the black-headed heron *Ardea melanocephala*. Discreetly coloured, its beauty resides in the fine markings of its grey coat.

 Flamboyant in its metallic coat and bright red beak, this malachite kingfisher *Alcedo cristata* is on the lookout for some small fry in the limpid waters of the river. The Okavango region is a favoured habitat of kingfishers and no fewer than eight species, each more beautiful than the last, can be encountered here.

 A saddle-billed stork *Ephippiorhynchus senegalensis* stalks the banks of a stagnant tributary of the Okavango. Impossible to confuse with any other bird, this splendid wader did not pause to indulge the photographer.

 The farthest reaches of the Okavango are sometimes difficult to explore because the vegetation is so dense; the cutting sedges, the gigantic papyrus and the entangled reeds combine to present almost insurmountable obstacles. Only by following one of the myriad of channels can one penetrate deep into the Delta.

 The tawny eagle *Aquila rapax* is a common raptor, be it in the most arid regions of the Kalahari or on the banks of the Okavango.

I have never come across as many different species of birds of prey as in this region of Africa. The raptor check-list for Botswana numbers no fewer than seventy-one species, diurnal and nocturnal. This is one of the more remarkable specimens: the bateleur *Terathopius ecaudatus*.

 Meeting with the leopard *Panthera pardus* is always a moment of heightened emotion. In Botswana this nocturnal cat is officially protected, but protection is enforced in only a few controlled areas. Elsewhere, it falls prey to poachers who hunt it for its skin. In certain regions, for example near the Tuli Block in the south-east, livestock farmers are sworn to its destruction.

 Although thunderstorms in the Okavango region are spectacular — and some can be violent — they do not generally affect the water level in the Delta. Rain falling in the Delta area serves only to make the roads impassable and temporarily fill the water-holes. The level of the Okavango depends totally on the nature of the rainy season in the Angolan highlands.

 The best way to explore the Delta is by *mokoro*, or wooden dugout canoe. The slow flow of the river allows for easy navigation.

 It is said that one cannot find purer water than that of the Okavango Delta. The white sands and extensive reed-beds through which the water drains act as natural filters, and in most areas the water can be drunk straight from the river.

 It is in the clear waters of the Okavango that the goliath heron *Ardea goliath* likes to fish. This giant among the waders of the Delta sometimes catches fish that are longer than forty centimetres. Its patience is unlimited: it can remain at the same fishing spot the whole day long.

 A waterbuck *Kobus ellipsiprymnus* ventures into the reeds. Most of the members of the genus *Kobus* live exclusively in damp areas. The male of the species grows to a height of 1,35 metres and can weigh up to 270 kilograms. In spite of its size, this antelope is relatively easy prey for the lions of the Delta.

 A wild dog *Lycaon pictus*, one of the most persistent and tireless hunters in Africa. The dogs will take turns in pursuing their prey which is savaged until it is eventually pulled down and killed by being torn apart. Although this might seem a vicious method of killing, the process is normally quick and little suffering is involved as the victim is believed to go into a severe state of shock.

White pelicans *Pelecanus onocrotalus* are excellent gliders, capable of soaring through the air like vultures. In Botswana they are found only around the permanent waters of the Okavango, Lake Ngami and the Chobe.

The lechwe *Kobus leche* has a population of some thirty thousand spread between the Okavango Delta and the Zambezi Basin. Its future seems to have been secured by the efficient protection of the Delta and it is in fact in this region that the largest number of this very specialized, water-loving antelope can now be found.

Hippopotamuses *Hippopotamus amphibius* are always present in the Delta. If you are travelling through the Okavango it would be wise to choose a guide who knows where they are likely to be encountered; they could be dangerous.

An amorous display by a couple of giraffe *Giraffa camelopardalis* in the Moremi Wildlife Reserve. These extraordinary creatures will drink when water is available but are not dependent on it; in Botswana they may be found in the most arid areas of the Kalahari as well as on the fringes of the Delta.

The Moremi Wildlife Reserve is the only part of the Delta that can be covered by vehicle — preferably one with four-wheel drive. The Reserve is situated on a peninsula, the vegetation of which is wooded savanna. It is dotted with water-holes and pans and the larger game animals are plentiful here.

The darter *Anhinga melanogaster* is certainly one of the strangest birds of the Delta. Its silhouette, more hydrodynamic than aerodynamic, is ideally suited to diving, swimming and fishing. Like the cormorants, to which it is related, it pursues its prey underwater with astonishing speed.

In some places in the Reserve, the tributaries of the Okavango penetrate into the reed-beds. Here one can experience the idyllic charms of a small paradise, like this minute lagoon covered with waterlilies and surrounded by papyrus.

The cattle egret *Bubulcus ibis* perched on the back of this old male buffalo has hit upon a novel way to cross a tributary of the Okavango.

Hippopotamuses spend about half their lives in the water. At night they emerge to graze along the banks of the Okavango.

The elephant herds of the Delta are sometimes impressive. Certain water-holes are known for the hundreds of animals that visit each day.

The peninsulas of dry bush that jut into the Okavango wetland are elephant territory. Water is vital to the survival of these animals. Large numbers of elephant *Loxodonta africana*, in total numbering perhaps 40 000, are concentrated in the north of the Kalahari between the Okavango Delta and the Zambezi Basin.

The beginning and end of the day are the best moments to experience the wild. Both animal and observer appreciate the coolness of the air.

The beautiful tusks of this animal are coveted by poachers, who are still active in certain areas of the Okavango. Crocodiles and elephant are the main prey of poaching traffic in the uncontrolled regions of Botswana.

Disturbed by the presence of an observer, a waterbuck *Kobus ellipsiprymnus* stands quietly behind the camouflaging bushes.

The elephant population of the Okavango and its neighbouring regions is still healthy: food is abundant, water is always available and the wild stretches are big enough to support a large number of animals. Farther to the north, in the Savuti region adjacent to and east of the Moremi Wildlife Reserve, the elephants have suffered from the effects of drought over the last few years.

Bibliography

Balsan, F. *L'étreinte du Kalahari*, Boivin

Balsan, F. *Le capricorne noir*, Société continetale d'éditions modernes illustrées, 1968

Battistini, R. *L'Afrique australe et Madagascar*, Paris, 1967

Botswana - National Parks and Reserves, Botswana, Division of Tourism, Gaborone

Brown, L. *L'Afrique*, Hachette, Paris

Campbell, A. *The Guide to Botswana*, Winchester Press, Gaborone, 1968

Dorst, J. and Dandelot, P. *A field guide to the larger mammals of Africa*, Collins, London, 1983

Game Parks and Nature Reserves of Southern Africa, Reader's Digest, Cape Town, 1983

Johnson, P. and Bannister, A. *Okavango, Sea of Land, Land of Water*, Struik, Cape Town, 1977

Livingstone, D. *Missionary Travels and Researches in South Africa*, Murray, London, 1857

Murray, M.L. *Present Wildlife Utilisation in the Central Kalahari Game Reserve* Department of Wildlife, National Parks, Gaborone, 1967

Owens, M. and D. *Cry of the Kalahari*, Collins, London, 1985

Maclean, G.L. *Roberts' Birds of Southern Africa*, John Voelcker Bird Book Fund, Cape Town, 1985

Smithers, R.H.N. *The Mammals of the Southern African Subregion*, University of Pretoria, 1983

Tinley, K.L. *Moremi Wildlife Reserve*, Okavango Wildlife Society, 1966

Wellington, J.H. *Southern Africa: A Geographical Study*, London, 1955